www.finishinglinepress.com

Maps To The Vanishing

poems by

Nate Maxson

Finishing Line Press
Georgetown, Kentucky

Maps To The Vanishing

The front cover of this book is a map of the forests of Transylvania dated 1886.

The map on the back cover's origin is more obscure. It appears to be a somewhat inaccurate, pre revolution Russian map of Vladivostok, likely from during the Russo-Japanese War as it has Japanese writing and diagrams of what appear to be shipping lanes and what may be artillery positions drawn in red ink with more writing in purple covering over the original Cyrillic letters. It may be a Russian map that was somehow obtained by the Japanese military or intelligence during that conflict. Vladivostok is also where my paternal great grandfather was imprisoned for a number of years after World War 1.

Publisher: Leah Huete de Maines
Editor: Christen Kincaid
Author Photo: Nate Maxson
Cover Design: Elizabeth Maines McCleavy

Order online: www.finishinglinepress.com
also available on amazon.com

Author inquiries and mail orders:
Finishing Line Press
P. O. Box 1626
Georgetown, Kentucky 40324
U. S. A.

Table of Contents

I. Landscapes

"The lie is the future, one may venture to say [...]. To tell the truth is, on the contrary, to say what is or what will have been and it would instead prefer the past."

—Jacques Derrida, "Without Alibi"

Overture With Atlas And Joy Division

I was gifted an old atlas, 1829: maps of the ancient world according to the younger old world/ half the pages slipped from the spine but intact, blueprints/ each ink shade ground from a different live subject, chromolithography, graphite stone for black, mummy brown and the blue of insectile wings/ this is the way/ Latin names for a made up world/ step inside/ just like we make them up/ just like they make us up, dream us/unaware landscapes of unknown Europes inside The Dreamtime reaching/ this is the way, step inside/ this is the way, step inside

Cinderland

I would prefer to leave the mystery open, like a beating wound (a doorway)
Like a furnace that sings to the fields in daylight

Let us consider the miraculous from a distance
Like the time between the first photograph of the earth from space
And the first man to make a crop circle in his cornfield and then call the media
Perhaps the way they'd demand an exorcist from the church during plague-
years
A hunger for somewhere other, just elsewhere, a new rain

Here, one night a long time ago: when they shut down *all* the mental hospitals
and let everyone go
Doors open to streetlamps benevolently silhouetting escapees shuffling through
the trees

You're free to go
The wet grass greener than it had ever been
The perfect blue of swimming pools

After Saint Mark's Bronze Horses In Venice,
Where I've Never Been

A certain holding close of one's breath (like a buttonless jacket in the cold) is bound to happen when passing below the-bridge-of-sighs, one of many: hogs to the long slaughter preserved on an apricot pit sharp edge

Our bare feet gliding over hunger stones placed to appear when the river gets low, cityscape steaming on the water
Where bronze horses displayed in the plaza seem to turn at dusk like a sundial in reverse: photograph of a fire curling and vanishing into white air
You can picture though: the sacking of the city, where they placed a crucifix on a hill with a plaque to commemorate the winners

Stone lapped with wind/ I cross myself, or rather my shadow, the motion: North Star, then South, then right and left, and to finish it you spit theatrically
An ornamentation to distance the eventual
I have been nowhere/ but this/ desert
I am a stripped nowhere hauled in from the east on the backs of flatbed trucks
I am a nowhere horse poured in gold to catch the light

Filament

That split in time when you were young and rushing to turn out the lights in a room when you left it, an attic or a garage, that kind of thing: noctophobia, fear of the dark, the first seam popped and never sewn back

When you turn out the light, the room fills with your days

All the rooms with all the days, here they are

Lying on the floors like corpses looking up at the sky through holes in the ceiling, teeth coated in glimmering lapis lazuli, a burial ritual they won't understand when they find it, yucca moths having eaten away the shrouds

The rooms fill with days like water, until you can't open most of the doors in the house anymore, out of fear of the days flooding out

I tiptoe past the locked facades, cat burglar silent

What fills the world/ bulb/ pool/ room/ what fills the space when you look away

Rococo

A catalogue of the vaults:
The first item we come to, dredged up out of cobwebs and filmstrips
Amber ossification occurring strictly in the light which we don't let touch us,
A medieval painting of all 12 apostles
Each with an unfinished novel, the length of which is indicated by the bitterness
of his smile
All with the same subject matter,
"Girls in books that haven't been written yet and the unsettlingly far older men
who love them"

Every generation wants to be the last one
Down in the depths, where the flashlight's beam (long after we ceased yelling
for rescue) begins to come back round
Because it is a circle
The angel of death looks just like you or I
But made of a more *solid* substance than flesh or al fresco
The world-cancer
What we are convinced we deserve
What will make us whole

Their hands reach to the sky and gesture at a rainbow
It took the artist twenty years to finish

Just the hands

So delicate
If you look away/ they disappear

Map Of Isola Di Pantelleria (Half Sung)

A temporary coagulation: wind land
This desire for the near zero, horizonal: *Riemann's zeta function*
No grasp of the temporal but to swim
Moving towards it but never arriving
The Giardino Pantesco: old stone, obsidian cairns ringed over single trees for
trapping the fog
Daylight's vapor turned to rain
The other side of the world we still think of in 2D terms,
Low tone/ last song
Far island crags/ 300 miles from Tunisia/ places that you dream but never see
Patches of wiry dead grass breathing in the blue nocturnal
An assumption of home, of return: not when but where
A magic trick hidden in hand motions and wolf prints in the mud, faked to
scare the neighbors
On this hill where we can briefly see
Down below, a little city, lights in every window, all going out like stars

Homeopathy

Divination by fire, I like to watch the embers reaching out of the pit/ what does one see in the flames? Brutus, taking the fastest horse out of Rome/ taxidermy jaguars in museums with eyes made of turquoise/ alchemical principles, occultations/ they would burn witches to gather the clouds in the event of drought or crop failure/ someone to blame/ like arrows tipped with silver nitrate, homeopathic, smoke to bring the rain

Tower Of Babel

The scientific theory of ghosts
Isn't what you think it is
It's much more simple actually
To make a house haunted
You just repeatedly say, that it's haunted
And wait
It's a kind of measurement, not too complicated if you make sure not to look too closely
Like the iron bars in France they kept in a vault to make sure there was no question about how big a meter was
Only one true measurement, it stayed like that until the 1950s, after an attempt at standardization
How far do you think it is though? If you were to squint…
Can you see the land on the other side of this vast water?
How many, hand over foot, rods of iron would it take to cross the landscape?
Iron and salt in a circle around one's bed to keep the spirits away
When revolutionary French scientists decided *this* was the measurement, their answer to, "how do we know?" was, "because this is the measurement and we only had to question it once"
Or, while we're engaging in classical mathematics, how much iron do you think resides in the bloodstream?
Not enough, not enough
The function of spirit in time, all magic being stage magic if you're not careful
It's Clarke's third law in reverse,
How we're trained to pray in the archaic familiar, *thy* kingdom come, never you or yours
I've whispered the attempt into the architecture, into the foundation of the structure, this is what you do, to make a ghost, you speak its name
And then you let the world encase it, the eggshell grown over soft yolk
This is a birth-story, like the kind the women humblebrag while tallying each others' wounds by hand
How we're trained to ask without expecting an answer:
What came first?
The world or the stone?

Scale Model

From high enough up it's a question of scale
The mountains look like campfire skeletons,
Left over from the last earth's burning
      And this is where you *will* the wind
      And this is where you will know gravity
      And this is a failure of silence
Only witness to the act in preparation
A man talked down from a bridge by police with guns drawn
      What we remember as we strap on these wings
How, as a child I would pop clover blossoms into my mouth from the grass
In hopes of tasting what the bees taste before the honey
      Is it smoke or rainclouds that create such a shade of Edwardian gray,
Cinders or embers? What I carry in the angry womb of my memory
A bird's eye view, I am a dying fall, a ventriloquism act
The voices when they call me, call me into flight

The Little Ice Age

Antonio Stradivari made his violins from trees whose wood was thickened from the cold/ who went out into the wild for him? Cut down the trees with long saws, hauled them off on horse drawn carts to Milan? We can count the rings, on the bodies of the instruments/ see the heaviest ones/ for the coldest years/ the most pure tone

Fireland Picaresque

The cinderland turns to a fireland
On the axis
A resurrection
The rainy season
A blackbird and an ashbird
On different sides of a coin
Ambiguous hulkage of frost and fur
Stalks like a black hold
Through the kindling reeds

The Divine Cartography

After the publication of Dante's Inferno, medieval Italy went through a craze for infernal geography, that is: the mapping out, of hell/ grand maps in ink on parchment detailing the underworlds/ to map the world before we know the world/ it's the labyrinth growing from a maze into a city into a hollowed out landscape/ we are only the outermost sphere/ we dream of warm water, glow-in-the-dark fish/ and the oceans we haven't yet named

II. Doubled Images

"This world—
to what may I liken it?
To autumn fields
lit dimly in the dusk
by lightning flashes."

—Minamoto Shitago, death poem, circa 983CE

Monsoon/ Ligament

To correlate objects in time, a pattern out of a few stray sounds like an atonal flautist just outside the limit of adult decibels
Here:
A road covered in finches killed by a hailstorm
We can try
To build a narrative out of what amount to rushes poking briefly above the river as it swells
An Afghani woman with glass eyes, her head covered in a maroon hood: the way the light shined in them through flashbulbs from an old camera (a famous photograph in National Geographic easily substituted for empathy)
The connective tissue between memory and flood: an approach
I will stitch the echoing sinew: what surfacing objects are apparent
The birds fall out of the sky but you never get to see them fall
The thick magazine on top of a dumpster, pages curling and ink blots welling up like a slow surgery
Falling exists in hindsight (the repetition of an idea, a ripple)
The animal splayed in a white stigmata
Only aftermath, the water breathes one way and then the other
Quieter now than when I wanted to prove my accuracy,
My ability to bear witness
By swallowing until some piece of detritus from the monsoon stuck in my throat

Emily/ Litany

For years I thought that the flowers called black-eyed susans were black -eyed *bruises*
As in "I don't like the way Black Eyed Bruises smell"
Sometimes these things come to me in the ebb tide of my aphasias, these spoonerisms
Little flickers balking against the wind in a candelabra
Have you ever noticed the varying but similar iconographic depictions of saints between the Roman Catholic Church and that of eastern holy men among the various religious authorities of India?
One depicts the saints with halos while the Buddhas and the Krishnas have a more ambiguous candle flame wavering above their heads
It usually appears to burn counterclockwise
As a not particularly religious but ever so observant Jew, I pay attention to these things
The difference between the light and the fire
While I watch out the window after smelling smoke, so expectant
What a sad day it is that the FBI are going through what used to be Emily Dickenson's front garden with drug sniffing dogs looking for discarded crack pipes and needles, foregone conclusions really
Anything to posthumously take away her medals in light of potential disgrace, that's the way of the world in this future
Tell me another
When given a choice between a certainty and only the potential of consumption (paper curling in a hearth)
Which would you prefer as your chosen method of combustion?
Think carefully now
There is a phrase we used to use to describe such situations:
The lady or the tiger?
The flowers all get bruises or the spinsters get the pyre

Wingspan/Post-Flight Measurements

A vast act of remembrance, this
The Blizzard Forever, 1989 to 2017 (so far)

You hardly notice
The wingspan spreading overhead
I assume
A deliberateness to the motion

Dark water in small amounts
That's your vaccination
Against exposure, against the cold
Folded like a failed Polaroid

It *could* be a dream
I'm in conversation with
But whose?
There's no great comfort
In the sterile clockwork mathematics of all this
Of course the machinery could be perfected eventually
But it's less interesting than leaving the grit inside to eat up the gears
I prefer to think in terms of catastrophe, in terms of thirst
A choral ode, a downturn: saltwater in a moon-white teacup
Mistaken for light and sipped with a civilized grimace
Whatever it is that makes you feel better
The etymology will be painfully obvious
Most of the time I measure it in dents and bruises
Compared to the last crash landing
What heals tallied next to what doesn't
Except on some dusks when I am spectral, uninhibited and wounded
X-rayed till I hiss:
A slow dancelike, movement in the thinning shade alone
This way
The divide
Before it disappears,
Before a world begins
A déjà vu is etched in sudden snow

Light Pollution/ Ariadne

A skull and bones wing-pattern coat jumps
Lives, running inside a flicker
Flight evolved out to a memory,
A rediscovery
All across the American veldt
The eyes of those who looked
Too long into daylight
Are rolling back white in their heads
The stars are disappearing
To light pollution
(a toast)
They say
You could once see the Milky Way galaxy
Zoom in from that wide lens,
That general negation
To a motion that sparks and sways
To watch what moves across the streetlamp
Like a spotlight on a stage
One breath and then it's gone
Arrhythmia and the labyrinth
An optical illusion
But a convincing one
A hieroglyph of matches
Erasure
Of what you used to see
It's a slow death
A macular degeneration
Lit by children
We know it
The way we know without saying it
That all dogs are born, orphans
When we see a shape hopping shadowy
Across the empty, tumbleweed filled canals
These long legged nights of the drought
Color blind snipers
Firing into the dark

Mosaic/ Mandala

Just 30 seconds into the past and things are finally starting to wake up
In this entanglement of mathematics and silt
My forest is a theory
Somewhere
An exercise in deep green
I learned a new word today: abacomancy, a method of divination through
smoke
That's what I've been practicing in
Watch which way the shapes drift
Cloud formations shaped by translucently small hands
So what have we got when all is said and done?
Are we in the red or are we in the black?
What are we, as the aphorism goes: throwing against the wall with the hope
that it sticks?
Bull's blood/ boy's sweat/ the formaldehyde reaction/ to vanish like foam on
the waves
My forest lit for a signal
My burbling swoon into its illuminated bramble of purgatorio manuscripts
A motion, a method
The ripe eventual
In absentia dreaming

Evening Wear/ Three Masks

A dark sky sanctuary/ where they don't let the light in without a permit
In earlier days the philosophers talked of angels and needles and endangered
species
All the self-important people who say they built the world
Now it's all something about: how many ghosts will *fit* inside the machine?

The first time we ever touched the moon
A clown car paradox
While we're still laughing

A still field
When the sun's going down
Windless
At night
I never feel the cold

Astrolabe/ Autoclave

Rivers named in pre-Latinate languages vanish along with the words for them
It's possible to follow them (from the middle)
And see them go vaporous into the salt and dust
Having only an awareness of a vague center
But the following of it
No one ever does that completely
Even though it's what you're supposed to do,
Be a big shot, use the right tools: mapping it all out
Idolizing the stock image of Dante driving on an interstate which is gradually
sloping down
Yes, yes: all that is very nice
But does the city really dream?
To build a railway for the dead and never see its end
Who dreams each spike and each nail?
The word escapes me like a sudden anosmic taste of rye whiskey and steam

Shipwreck/ Citizenship Test

Black mountains disappearing and reappearing,
Venetian funeral boats bob in and out while the big one sinks

I would like to digress now from starry eyed funereal planning and talk about
the other subject I've talked about quite a lot recently: people who return from
disappearance, a magic trick: Amelia Earhart's bones used in a ritual to tell the
future/ the speech in which an Irish prime minister used the phrase "comely
maidens dancing at the crossroads" (a misquotation but who cares), the animal
of unknowing: nature's perfect predator/ it's the vanish and the return that form
the motion of an offset circle/ twilight among the Begonias, the state flower and
the desert/ Colonel Kurtz and Jesus Christ and all their retainers/ in a long
enough timeline, fiction disappears/ the top google search regarding William
Shakespeare is, "were Romeo and Juliet real?" because at a certain point we
simply accept that the founders of Rome were suckled by wolves/ it's like a wave
function: time, compressing up to the present moment and then spilling back
out into another empty forever like the place where the rivers empty into the
sea while the seas quietly empty back into the sky/ my island, my America, if
you can't tell whether I'm weeping or chuckling: don't ask because the answer
will disappoint you/ I'm going to snap my fingers a second time and let this
charade continue burning until it gutters out or blisters my hands/ the island
where I come from is sinking into brine and reappearing on the other side

So,
When they ask me, with a black bag over my head so I can't cheat
What I know about the country called the past
Where I'm supposed to desire
A return
Most days
Compared to this
I'll say:

Charlie Chaplin's eyes were blue
And Ovid is on the water
Noticing the fog

Labyrinth/ Floodland

Put your arms out in front of you to feel along the walls, every fifty feet there
will be a metal stud—knock gently to hear it—you can use these to find your
way back to the island, the aperture, an escape mechanism
The same way that, when a sea turtle dies
You can count the rings on a bone in its neck to tell its age, like a tree
Or how hummingbirds typically expire in their sleep, starvation setting in after
a few hours without nectar
I trace the lines and future-ruts on my face: daily, several times a day and in
several different mirrors (our cliché, the humming of a dramatic pop song on
the radio between commercials when we used to listen)
Like footpaths and holloways carved by years of organic traffic: visible in
hindsight, a scarification
A cultivated labyrinth, what hides among the endangered flora and fauna
growing slinking along the architecture
A repetition of all the different ways there are to dream and drink without going
in too deeply to the rivers of Lethe with its life sized crucifixes and cattails and
lightning rods all peeking their heads above the high tide
You can hold these facts out in front of you like lights against the water while
it rushes in

Trajectory/ Shadow

What's missing is too subtle for the euphemism:
"Phantom limb syndrome"
I walk into a room, negative space of what was there
A hole in the middle of what I remember

It's like the people who say, "My father built this house"
The shadow to the word is that they did not,

So I alternate a live current
Between the spirit and the muscle
Blue and red,
The shadow of the sound and the shadow of the weight
The Atlas organ, if we're being pedantic about it
A Wi-Fi router attached to a spine
An evolution dear to the pit

Descend endlessly
And never fall

III. Divinations

"'Memory's images, once they are fixed in words, are erased,' Polo said. 'Perhaps I am afraid of losing Venice all at once, if I speak of it. Or perhaps, speaking of other cities, I have already lost it, little by little.'"

—Italo Calvino, "Invisible Cities"

The Pale Horse Illusion Explained

A magic lantern (early memory storage) casts its gravity on a slaughterhouse wall, skinned pigs strung like Noh theater shadows
When we are in the after, may I then speak of this? Am I allowed? Are the lights just temperate enough?
Just right, not the coins in the wishing well but the wishes: liquid and swift
I dream this, the end of a film, and it dreams me back: my childhood dog sniffing at puddles of antifreeze glowing like winter (there, again, light projected towards me: an optical illusion in two directions)
All the creatures that populate the distant labyrinth, lift their heads from watering holes in the blind
I'm getting too big to fit through the cracks, not all of me, not anymore: just the eyes in witness rather than the entire weight
Ambiguous creature whose clockwork knees crack like hail storms, is it getting closer or further away? A ship bobbing in and out of being, on the horizon of the grasslands

July 1999

An ageless wind that shakes the plains, moving tidally inland on our houses and gardens
Here, where I am a child hiding with my family and our neighbors in the barn, the red barn, red like barns are supposed to be...
We had shot fireworks off into the sky
As if they summoned the funnel clouds and the sound
Separate entities and offerings
The dust filtering down onto us, prayerlike quiet like a bomb shelter
Those of us who held the spark of our childhoods into the new century were granted a second birth
Those of us born to the new sky
Nascent moonland, let me live again
Windland let me dream
Smoke trails reaching and falling towards high off cranes
This hour between time when you redreamed the world in grace

The Mirror Tarot: Cold Reading

The Elephant Graveyard
A major arcana
A bonfire licking at the night sky's soft blue underside
Men with gloved hands warm themselves on its border
Faces smoky and scarved

When they catch the poachers
They burn them like witches on pyres of ivory

That one is for the past

Now the present moment enters the frame

The Queen Of Lilies
This is your card
Her face emerges
Unscratched from a bramble
In each hand she has an apple
Then the branches close in and her face vanishes
Cheshire cat-like
She closes each hand and the apples blink out too
Hands withdraw
Only a breeze

Try to remember
Where those gold apples bloomed to the touch

Now the future: muddiest of all the waters
Seven Of Crows
A floating city
Where no one talks
It's Venice in reverse
It lifted off the ground one day
Rose an inch a year
Grew like a child
That way
They hope the crows

Eventually
Pull them back to earth
Like so much smoke
Where a large shape went crashing
Through the trees

Fathom

What you can see in the sky on a clear day
What we could see but don't
In the water backwards, an Ophelia pose
Moonlike daylight apparition
A constellation shaped like Gorbachev's birthmark
And the ghost of the tallest waterslide ever constructed,
Torn down after the death of a child
Shuffle these signs like a three card monte and see what happens
Oracle marks carved like teething dents on turtle shells,
Set upside down to float down the river with candles that quickly burn out
Here is the ritual over your eyes like a veil
Event horizon,
How we know the world is round even when the object disappears

A Lever For The Days

Cue
See the click of a pen touched in thought to the teeth
A day will come
See the sandhill cranes in flight
They migrate from Siberia, an endangered species
All the days
All the days will come
See the steam from a teacup
Too hot to sip, but blow on it
Create little waves,
Green tea whitecaps to speed on the process

Artifact
Snow over the highway
New Mexico
February, 2004 I think it was?
A knee deep settled storm
Enough to shut down traffic
"Will you tell me the last time you felt free?"
There will come a wind across the grasslands
Sun on white
Gleam and melt
You will find the gates of your life-size prison camp,
Opened to scattered birdsong
The world unfurling and furling like tapestry and spool
When was the last
Time
Every day
Turned over in my hands
Brightness and eventual

Introductions

When I was seven years old my friend Travis who lived across the street took me into his garage to show me the deer his father had killed on a hunt which was hanging upside down, blood dripping out into a drain

I was fascinated, it was my first real death
I reached over and touched the cool, stiff fur,
It swung slightly as if in a breeze
I felt the protrusion of its antlers, one of which was just inches from the concrete floor

Travis explained to me, with great enthusiasm, how he and his father would strip the hide after the blood was drained and keep the horns and have venison steaks and jerky

My father has never killed anything and at the moment I felt almost shameful because of it
A line of warped scripture that I didn't know how I knew came to me
"Forgive us you animal for we know exactly what we do"
That still comes to me sometimes
Even as my memories yellow like newspaper or perhaps ivory in some places and coalesce around certain bright spots
I still have this, odd bloody gem: the buck hanged like The Hanged Man on a tarot card
For months I dreamed it swinging from the sky
Forgive us
We know
What kind of prayer would "let me live in this world" be anyway?

Modernism

Something moves across the road without touching
Or alternatively *the road* is jumped over
Depending on your definition of bifurcation, what it means to map a vein in
the earth
That which we do not know
Tall enough to pass over
Head in the clouds
What haunts us?
The unknown animal,
The blanked book, ink ran to black in the rain
Alternate definitions of historical termination points/ *The White Cliffs of
Dover/ the continental railroad's last spike/ and Kafka's three sisters who died in
the camps*
The most popular forest on the island, for suicides and lovers alike
We assume
A leap of faith out of shadow
Where the trees grow
Crowding in
Close enough to speak

The Mirror Tarot: Unsafe Wiring

The Twins:
This is my card
It depicts Hercules in the underworld
Only his mortal shade though
The divine part
Split like an atom
Which part remembers?
One underground
        Stays behind to warn Odysseus on the shoreline of Tartarus
And one above
The earth is a mirror beneath our boots

The Snowshoe hare:
This is your card
Its mouth is ringed red from an unknown trespass
On a slower animal
                Nose twitch/ lick lips/ how they move
Small footprints in the snowdrift
A pastoral vanishing
Like Hemingway's baby shoes
An urban legend
The only evidence

Last card: Gehenna
The echo and the daylight
The dust
Ovens so big and so seldom fired
There are black birds nesting in the crooks

The Arms Race

There is a continuum of deathbed bon mottes at play in the phrase "in due time"
A tradition
Of who gets to be the sharpest

"More light more light"—Goethe's last words

If you ever look at a wrecking ball up close
You'll notice there is no welding line
They are cast from molten steel not forged
Not beaten into being but birthed for the sky
Like an egg made of silver, seamless

When is time due?

In the days before the X-ray machine
A doctor might hold a vibrating tuning fork
To the possibly broken bone
If it hurt like hell, that's how you found out

And to whom is the time owed?
The unnamed? The denamed?
Those burning in the desert?

"More weight, more weight",
Said the only *man* to be killed in the Salem witch trials
Refusing to confess as they piled on the stones

Several Images Of My Mother Who, Despite Poetic Convention, Is Not Dead

What do we remember?
The object or the reconstruction
The storm of the century or the story of it
Desert roses, unbloomed and hard
How, once when I was small
I caught my foot in a mudhole in a field
How scared I was of being dragged under
When my mother pulled me away
I had lost the shoe

How she told me years later that when *she* was young, in Israel
She used Kabalistic numerology to decipher God's phone number
But never called it
It made me think of that lost shoe, that trite signifier
With its bright colors and its Velcro

I always picture her in the winter
How she broke her tailbone on a sled
That disintegrated going downhill with me on her lap
A class action lawsuit, I think, ensued
Those days are a white blur

How I cannot remember her and my father
Before their divorce
Ever expressing any affection to one another
How one year for Hanukkah
She built a huge menorah decoration
Out of chicken wire and duck tape and blue lights
Planted it on the front lawn on Christmas Eve
I watched it from the window
As a blizzard came down and the lights never flickered

The Kafka phrase "an axe for the frozen sea" comes to mind
With the picture (unclear if it's a dream or a memory)
Of my mother at the wheel of a car in the west
Wiping away the fog of her breath
Hunched and gripping the wheel against a storm

A roar both sound and light
Against some great dark at the glass
At bay
But trudging
Forward

Frost Fair

I've never been really east
What I call east would make them laugh
I would go east in time, like so
To fly at the speed of time is to reach a stasis
The last frost fair of 1814 when the Thames froze over
And they marched an elephant across the surface
Before the thaw, what would you be willing to burn?
The myths we tell ourselves
About the old world
While the new one gathers kindling

The Mars Rover Sings Happy Birthday To Itself

A teaspoon of dark matter,
What I'm here to gather in my eventuality
All the pianos nobody ever learned to play
Are a theory the mass of a white sun
Their equations in my gears
What I can sing with, without a voice
Compressed to an ivory clatter
In a space as big as—*something in my eye*
I'm calculating the weight
Of a red night sky written in disappearing ink
The heft of it,
Looping and turning
Like ashfall or bats in the spring
A grand hibernation in the rearview mirror,
Now the red land comes awake
An engine vanished into the air
And the blood black,
Ebony vein
The vapor trail is soon to follow

The Echo

Do you remember how when you were a child
In a cavernous space
You would say "echo"
To test the echo?
That was what you would say
"Echo"

Now when I speak into space
It's usually a selfish prayer of some kind

Oh blank noise
Let me die with my mystery intact

The Mirror Tarot: Still Life

A blood orange peeled and then set down
Shining like an organ on a plate
You can see the shadow of whoever did it, in the frame
Il Tarocco, you hold your breath when you pick one and can't say why
Object/ spirit/ light/ appearance
Caravaggio painting, inside the casket, on the inner lid and we'd never even know
The method of cultivation, for this succulent
Pollen-heavy bees and white grass that turns in the wind like a Japanese movie
Grown on an island where it's daylight for half the year, not north but south
What comes to you
Not a dream but now
A continental memory, when you bite down
The slight noise of your playing on a distant relative's piano
In a house last century, doesn't that seem strange to say?
Nobody ever played it but the children
The sound transfigured, fruit turned to paint
Dust caught in the eye of the machine that keeps the seeds

Waterloo

After the battle of Waterloo they say that Europe's false teeth supply was provided for decades on
From the mouths of its frozen dead
Before that they used ivory or wood or yes the occasional human tooth
But there'd never before been such a ready supply
I take this as fact
An act of transubstantiation: water to wine, that kind of thing
When does a real tooth become a false one?
It would require an army of dentists taking the field with pliers and mason jars, right?
You'd have to stand (like this) on the chest while squatting (bracing against it) to yank when you had your grip
All the people you've never seen
Napoleon and the Ancien Regime
Supply lines or supplies
One or the other
Speaking in tongues against the snow

Execution Koan

After Bertolt Brecht's "What Keeps Mankind Alive"

When I contemplate winter, and I have been for years
What keeps mankind alive? Asks the business casual national anthem, well
An object in a snow globe, a mondegreen
You separate time and keep it in your hands
Like a chunk of ice, post-blizzard (how we measure the days in here)
Unaware and hopelessly obvious
Like anatomically correct saints, served al fresco
Or pigs with human heart transplants
When I think of the cold,
What keeps the process going when it's briefly separated from the body
A false memory
Like how I swear I remember
Seeing Timothy McVeigh's execution,
The same day as my twelfth birthday
Broadcast live on network television
The effect of building such objects
Backwards and behind us,
These labyrinths
After this
It's where old maps would say
"Terra Incognita", unknown earth: the end of the century
When I contemplate the cold
When I assume the cold goes forever
Never gets tired, never flags
Never stops chasing you
Like cancer, like a boot wearing Freudian god, like losing interest in your toys
Half the world underwater
When I contemplate...
When I grab hold of what's inside
Smooth glass walls
How much is snow and how much is confetti?
This summer of 2001 where certain of my organs still live in the glow
My birthday, the execution date delayed forever
Somehow I remember the event, down to the static on the screen
Maybe

If you see red
Like a bull, like a boy
It means you're not
Color blind
Like summer
The outdated
Opposite number
Swallow, swallow
Bestial acts, stopwatches to time the surgery
To make sure where we put the heart stays chilled
The autoclaving of what we make, memory a step behind
A room full of silence
Is silent
Except
When it isn't

The Mystery Kingdom

Cryptophasia is the secret and individual languages of twins
But what of trees and hummingbirds?
We have an incomplete taxonomy for fading dreams and falling stars
For the singular being pluralized

Here, I have a quiet reverie
One would have to go back a century and cite Eliot with "death's dream
kingdom"
To try and pin it down, if one were to try
Here, ok, I'm a teenager and I'm in the bathtub
Biting my lower lip until it bleeds
Until it blooms a salt bright, jellyfish tendril down to my thighs and then *gone*
Like another self was there to observe and then ceased
This is the mystery kingdom
Who we are in its warm current

Incomplete
A bird in each hand (and yet not)
The genus of mystery
Of mirrors and why we cover them when we're in mourning
Who it was that built the city
Before the conquerors conquered the conquerors
And who the pyramid?
Before the buried buried the buried
And why the labyrinth? Why indeed
A stone for each of us
And a cairn for the living
A coiled blossom
Something more than the self and other tired objects
Wished upon as it burns up in the atmosphere
You would pray for an unidentified flying object,
The white dog in the desert who digs for rain

Lineage

There was a lightning rod on the roof of the first house I lived in when I was
in college
I would climb up to look at it on days when there were no clouds, years ago now
I regarded it like some tarnished silver idol
I knew the superstition that they drew the bolts *toward* them,
That they were mechanisms of summoning
Rather than the other way around
Which was why on the tip of the metal:
A little crystal ball was placed, welded
To mitigate the unknown
A snow globe in reverse
I only touched it once,
First the cool metal and then the clear glass nodule
Almost expecting it to be hot like a stovetop
I put my hand to the cold
And when I pulled away it stayed cold for a long time
As if I had absorbed some ringing hymn from inside the lightning rod
Some future illumination traveling at an impossible speed
From a sky I've never seen
It will mistake me for a piece of silver
And I will alight
For rooftops rumbling and high,
A hint of trembled blue
Hidden in my jacket like a memory
Of all the could-have-beens you've ever touched
Beginning to sing, at once

Borderlands Syndrome

You don't get away from being born on the borderlands
You just carry them with you, a keepsake under the skin: a static constant
The men of my family have always been cursed with this
And everyone can tell
Just looking at us
In the brief hours before we turn back into vapor,
Quoting cultish bible passages at inappropriate moments
Say we do dream purgatory,
Well then which one is it?
My body slobbered by fire
Or a steel fence cut through the suburbs?
Where the river diagonally meets the wall, it just keeps going
Dividing to dust
Answer quickly and in the form of a question
Please
Let us amnesia the lilies of the field

For My Second Theory Of Impermanence, I'll Need A Volunteer From The Audience

The faces of the saints on fire
      In renaissance oil or black and white film
And that of amateur porn stars
      Approaching release
Are reenactments for posterity,
Our very own Joans Of Arc

Pretending miraculousness is an art form,
An alchemy
With eyes closed for dramatic effect

      It's like,
You're grinding yourself away in the dark
Waiting for a moment between disappearance
And the fleshy spark of martyrs
But what did you expect?
In a nation founded by Spanish grand inquisitors
The mute difference lies
In how convincingly
You fake it

Relativity

It's like this: I'm eight years old and being thrown into the swimming pool, hoisted by a shadowy, sunblock scented figure
Into the air, the terror I feel in that moment before I hit the water is my first taste of reality since being born
In such moments something flashes like a thunderstorm before the eyes

What do you see when you're falling?
Does it let you see it at the end?
Maybe like so?

Picture Napoleon writing his own version of the Koran by candlelight in a tent somewhere inside the Russian winter
A violet he took from the Ukrainian Wild Fields when he passed through is pressed between the pages of an earlier draft
I hear him pushing the quill, tattoo deep, into the fat of my back
The common night terror of a man sitting on your chest

Time stretched like a rubber band, all potential energy

I am in an arsenic-wallpapered room far underground, the aftermath of a burial-quake
There are mud dauber wasps in the walls, I can tell from the hum
They are building me
A palace without light
For when my life begins

It's the unremarkable *fünf* that comes of lighting a gas stove with a match, the German word for five like the digits on a hand
Someone told me I'm still falling
Towards the chlorine blue
The band snapping back forever
Like this
All time
Is one time
In one time
You'll understand
When it's too late

This object in my hands
A melody,
A clock I'm trying to wind without having the key
So one thinks of cutting open the mechanism,
Thinks of leaving,
Bare into the wood
Is this what you call
A celestial body?
Letters burnt in Arabic and French
Still holding my breath
The water rushing in like a human shipwreck

The Insect Kingdom

Pinned to the walls under glass,
Or hiding under plaster stones and blacklights,
Some alive and some smoked out and frozen
The names of the collection almost create an illusion of prescience to the lay
weekend visitor

The Painted Lady Butterfly: born with wet wings,
The Blue Death Feigning Beetle…

Someone names the small things like they would the night sky

In my dream, all the eggs I tried to crack for breakfast were filled with blood
What does it mean?
—The Starbellied Orbweaver Spider—

If you meet The Buddha on the road
You'll know what to do

Two Landscapes

Horseland
Animal weight pressed against the membrane of extinction
Running, a dust trail DNA spiral,
Cracks in the hardpan after the rain dries
Two circles overlapped,
An eclipse
Or eyes opening
Squinting in the wind
A settled freeze
Water for the sand
Solidified like steam from the engine's nose rising

Fogland
The hours leak like helium
Into blue
Our memories
The peripheral,
This creature of such delicate heft
Long legs stepping on leaves/bramble/glass
You'll know it from the sound
Never seen among the trees
The world-hoof moving
In time to the dark
Landscapes and vanishing

Afterimage

A blood red moon twenty years ago
The same color,
How I pulled out most of my baby teeth prematurely
The sensation of an empty socket probed by the tongue
I stand in front of two windows at once, one to the prairie and one to the street
Now/ then
Frost/ moon
White/ red
Hand to glass, colored by the smoke of a wildfire
It's the heavenly clock Charlie Brown!
The wired mechanism strung from my mouth to the doorknob

Heat Death

The heat death of the neighborhood
Our nostalgia for safely canonized squalor,
Times Square in the 1970s
We keep it strictly in the tense of *then*
Little birds, flightless: washed up on the shore
Waiting for smiling celebrities with toothbrushes to come scrape off the oil
Feed us, the marooned
An echoing glow and the sound of unspecified insects
Or perhaps streetlights
A magic trick, anything you throw me will vanish
But I can't tell
One hum from another
But by all means
Break the glass
In case of rapture

Canticle Of Days And Faces

After Phillip Larkin, "Days"

The days in object-form
Are what the archaeologists would pull from me
Like silver teeth and burial rings
From the hands of a figure in a tomb
Like so
The days
They move like shadows of machines in flight
The way children will smash ants wantonly, for fun
All of this will go
The dissolution
If you squint you can see them
Running through the knee high prairie grass

It's how I would watch my former love while she slept
Or how she'd hold me when I awoke gasping from a night terror

What remains
A white bird on a gray desert sky
How we carry the wound like a covered mirror up the mountain

There they go
The days
Long legged animals a moment ahead and a moment behind
How she snorted crushed OxyContin off a mirror
The black well echoing all the things we've done

It's a witch's ritual
Pull off the sheet and point the mirror at the sun
My first kiss, a boy in grade school during the greatest game of hide and seek
ever

All these ghosts
A corona of candle-smoke

They never found me

I followed them down the halls, out of my hiding place and they never found me

How he was taken away when it was realized…

I have a theory though
If you could take all the time,
All the steps that you spent
Going to work, to school, to the grocery store, and so on
And put them somewhere else
How many times would it wrap around the earth?
How far into the stars could you go?

Faces emerge from the dust and rain
On the highway outside Denver
Music stopped, waiting at the intersection but afraid to move until it goes

A tarot reading was once given to me
The Fool, The Tower, Seven Of Swords
Four cards

Lastly, you who I'm always conjuring at
When you were in the dim light of a room with the blinds closed
You looked at me, on the edge of those days
With such an electric clarity
Rain (the same rain) roaring across the rooftops and gutters
A ringing in my ears and the stroke of your hand across my hair like a lullaby

They would stand and try to recreate the sky, their own sky (but always the same sky)
Another sky
Somewhere
All my days are flying away
I've got a headful of winds
On a still hour, balanced
They speak to me in staged whispers,
The days,
Leaving me
Running, massive, can't see their heads for their height

Loping across the sands, indifferent like dogs
The bones of their masters buried (the same bones, the same sand)
Deep and singing, reverberating, the echo of the hours through empty rooms
forever

After Van Gogh's "Peasant Burning Weeds", 1883

Someone's way out on the edge, see there? Not the dreamlands but the sleep-
lands, far as the eye can water: desert twinned with still life and stillborn blooms
I imagine plucking one and putting it in my hair, an act of shaky defiance and
against what? This? Lung disease and a dormant orchard's roots
Where faces blur and spark and we don't speak when there's a dust storm
passing
They are torching, with unknown instruments and shadowed hands, small
cairns of thistle and cornhusk
Smoked into an orange, oil derrick dry coughing skyscape, it's a riddle: *I am
burning*—a billow of letters, like holding a mirror to a deathbed mouth to check
for breath—*I am that which walks from tarnished mirror gallery to grinding
outskirts, while Vincent dries sunflowers in the twilight*

Hale-Bopp Comet 1997

The comet was visible in the sky for about 18 months but I only remember seeing it one time
It was the same night our dog had killed a pregnant rabbit in the back yard, its half formed kittens spun across the concrete driveway, black objects in the suburban blue glow, one of the adults, I can't remember who, put their hands over my eyes but I'd already seen, among other things, the sky

It's so quiet during astrological phenomena, the eclipse of 2017 was the same way, the birds think it's the night time and stop their singing
How quiet things were for a while there
I think about that, a lot now
Some trick of nostalgia, an optical illusion
The result of being so young
The pause between centuries, like how the sunsets following the eruption of Krakatoa were especially vivid for years afterwards, for the whole gilded age and the fin de siècle, even appearing in such works of art as Munch's "The Scream" and the landscapes of William Turner, orange fires on the horizon

The pre modern quiet
The primitive peace, whole empires of boredom and irony
Those born into it think such a stillness will last forever

If anyone ever asks me what the days between days were like
I'd say,
If I can still remember

The blinking surprise of walking out of a movie theater into a daylight that seems sharp enough to cut,
And those places in the mountains where the snow doesn't melt

Storm's Eye View

All the things you knew for a moment, then quickly forgot
Anecdotes and funny stories, the allegedly inspirational
Odd coincidences on the tip of your tongue
What'sa matter?
Did you think the days weren't keeping track too?
Keeping better track actually
Better than I ever did, halfheartedly leaving notes in unintelligible handwriting
Like time capsules assuming I'd eventually find them again

Here's one: think of it as an informal tarot card (incidentally also the theme of
our talk tonight if you hadn't noticed)

*Robert E Lee posed for a photographer in his uniform the very day Abraham
Lincoln was killed,*
*Victorian black umbrellas at the procession, the only color that could successfully
hide the streaks of coal smoke endemic to the era*

Here's another: Maybe this one shows the future if you're into that kind of thing

Two men getting married in a synagogue even though one is an atheist
It's always,
*It's always a middle place: heatwave picking up in the streets when they get in the
car, both in the same thin suits*
One gets a nosebleed, the other gets out a tissue for him and they laugh about it
*Overhead the magpies are wheeling, forming asemic gyres like writing in the
daylight*
I did look up, when they started, almost thought I could read them
These flight patterns turning in the dark,
Trace them with your fingers
Like a map of the known world on your husband's shoulders

A psychic moment, age 10, face pressed to the fogging glass of a moving vehicle
Vehicles are what we define the world through or haven't you noticed?
The days and centuries flying by like images you might interpret from tea leaves
It used to be horses
Even in your memory
But not for a long time

In the middle where it's winter
Where it's always winter
Snow made from old newsprint curled acid white
Burning pages adrift and gravitating
Like the asbestos they allegedly used in movies like "It's A Wonderful Life" and
"The Wizard Of Oz"
All the things you knew for a moment
What we might be willing,
What we might be willing to burn if it meant we could remember

Hauntology

The optimistic or the new age among us might call it a manifestation if it paid in cash, it trudges out of the swamp in your dreams like a beast from the sea, one claw waving a report card full of failing grades

A collective haunting, the Gashadokuro is its name in Japanese and it is a fusion of tragedies risen to terror: skeletal apparitions made from the amassed bones of those lost to famine, while we're being academic about it—we may as well contemplate the monster

A more subtle example than these clichés, is that of the first wolves and the first boars to leave the Chernobyl disaster zone in generations, how you can't eat the latter and neither has any fear of human hunters, they still carry a seed of radiation in their bellies but wild animals rarely live long enough for cancer, so we track their emergence anecdotally but still keep our ears pricked for howls or snuffling come sundown

A self-defense mechanism, how we craft a specter—the wings of monarch butterflies and death's head moths

Maybe the folkloric aspect is only visible in hindsight, like the Hubble telescope catching light a thousand year after its escape

My gathering the memories of snowstorms from the well of my childhood and holding them in my hands like tender blossoms drying between pages of books I never finished is a spark-like prayer to the blackout

Rouse it or let it sleep, let it continue, the eventual is only a funeral in the short term: if we wait long enough, its fruit will drip from our mouths and hands, blood to a garden like light to water—the ambiguous distance between myself and the ghost

Acknowledgments

Much gratitude is due to the editors, publishers, and readers, of the various magazines, blogs, and anthologies where many of the poems in this collection were first published

The Mojave River Review, *Cinderland* and *Trajectory/ Shadow*

Treehouse Arts, *After Saint Mark's Bronze Horses In Venice, Where I've Never Been* and *Heat Death*

Sublunary Review, *Filament* and *Two Landscapes*

Madness Muse Press, *Rococo*

Gyroscope, *Map Of Isola Di Pantelleria (Half Sung)*

Bombfire Lit, *Tower Of Babel, Hale-Bopp Comet 1997*, and *Relativity*

Panoplyzine, *Scale Model*

The Westchester Review, *The Little Ice Age*

Filling Station, *The Divine Cartography*

Anti Heroin Chic, *Monsoon/Ligament, Mosaic/ Mandala*, and *Frost Fair*

Your One Phone Call, *Emily/ Litany* and *Evening Wear/ Three Masks*

Rasputin: A Poetry Thread, *Wingspan/ Post-Flight Measurements*

Tiny Flames Press, *Light Pollution/ Ariadne, The Mirror Tarot: Cold Reading*, and *The Mirror Tarot: Unsafe Wiring*

Encore Lit, *Astrolabe/ Autoclave*

Dreampop Press, *Shipwreck/ Citizenship Test*

Armarolla, *Labyrinth/ Floodland*

The Basil O'Flaherty, *The Pale Horse Illusion Explained* and *For My Second Theory Of Impermanence, I'll Need A Volunteer From The Audience*

Levee Magazine, *July 1999*

Bowery Gothic, *Fathom*

Young Ravens Literary Review, *Introductions*

Tinge Magazine, *Modernism*

Smartish Pace, *The Arms Race*

Cirrus, *Several Images Of My Mother Who, Despite Poetic Convention, Is Not Dead*

The Revue Post, *The Mars Rover Sings Happy Birthday To Itself*

Star 82 Review, *The Echo*

Pilgrimage Press, *Waterloo*

Parhelion Magazine, *Execution Koan*

Synaeresis, *The Mystery Kingdom*

Foliate Oak, *Lineage*

Sweet Tree Review, *Borderland Syndrome*

Lotus-Eater Magazine, *The Insect Kingdom*
The Heavy Feather Review, *Canticle Of Days And Faces*
Acta Victoriana, *After Van Gogh's "Peasant Burning Weeds", 1883*
Ginosko, *Storm's Eye View*
Thimble Magazine, *Hauntology*

Nate Maxson is a writer and performance artist. The author of several collections of poetry, he lives in Albuquerque, New Mexico.